Seeking

Perspective

Weaving Spirituality and Psychology
in Search of Clarity

ROBERT J. WICKS

Author of
Living Simply in an Anxious World

PAULIST PRESS
New York/Mahwah

Acknowledgments:
Cover photo by Kathleen B. Bradbury.
Chapter 4, "Reaching Out . . . Without Being Pulled Down," is a slightly modified version of a paper entitled "Spirituality and Ministry," which originally appeared in the *Princeton Seminary* Bulletin, February 1991.

Copyright © 1991 by Robert J. Wicks

Library of Congress Cataloging-in-Publication Data

Wicks, Robert J.
    Seeking perspective: weaving spirituality and psychology in search of clarity/ Robert J. Wicks.
       p. cm.
    Includes bibliographical references.
    ISBN 0-8091-3234-6
    1. Spiritual life—Catholic authors. 2. Consolation. 3. Psychology and religion.   I. Title.
    BX2350.2.W527   1991
    248.4'01'9—dc20   91-11370
                                                      CIP

Published by Paulist Press
997 Macarthur Boulevard
Mahwah, New Jersey 07430

Printed and bound in the United States of America

Contents

DEDICATION

For the quietly prayerful people in my life ... those friends from near and far who, without fanfare or comment, have prayed for me and my work. Thank you.

Foreword

Lurking in the mind and heart of almost everyone and sometimes put into words by some is the refrain: "Oh, for the good old days." There is a yearning for a time when things were better. There is a wish for times less hectic and filled with stress. There is a desire to return to a world where order reigned, roles were clearly defined, and relationships were more fulfilling. Cutting to the quick of these nostalgic reflections, Emerson reminds us that this is the best of times if only we knew what to do with them.

Today this challenge is all the more forceful when we are faced with major cultural changes. Nothing remains the same for very long. No one seems to place much value on continuity. There are those who say that time is running out, that we have passed the point where our ecosystems might not be able to satisfy our basic needs. People are running in many directions, and few wonder what makes them run.

In the midst of all this chaos and change, the charismatic Mother Teresa of Calcutta reminds us that spirituality is not a luxury for the few, it is the simple duty of each of us. In Robert Wicks' book *Seeking Perspective*, we are confronted by a recognition of this message and given hope that our lives can be meaningful. He gives us an appreciation for the kind of persons we can become—given the fact that an integrated spirituality and psychology deals with the entirety of what we are and what we do. It brings together all the various aspects of our being in relationship with the Spirit of the Lord. Finally, it involves a process of continual change, conversion, and maturing as persons whose lives through baptism are eternal and spiritual.

By accepting the fact that we are *who* we are because we are *when* we are and *where* we are, he preserves us from a primitive and romantic illusion of what spirituality was "in the good old days." Through insightful, informative, and even inspirational examples from his own life as well as from the lives of others, he reviews the power faith has for us. He points out that religion, to be real, must result in a deeper awareness of our place in the world and that only a sexuality, blended with the best of the feminine and the masculine, will image all we are capable of becoming. Those forces, which impede our progress in being all that we can be, are examined and perceptive warnings are given to prevent distortion to the image of the God who dwells within.

Seeking Perspective continues a tradition found in Robert Wicks' other writings. What is remarkable about this book is the author's willingness to put into print not only the product of his own reflections, but also the interest he has in sharing a process in the final chapter through which readers may also discover truths and meanings significant for themselves. To this end, he reveals himself to be the consummate teacher, for he is not content simply to impart knowledge, but he invites others to come to their own understandings and convictions as well.

Melvin C. Blanchette

*"If therefore your eye is good,
your whole body will be good."*

Mt 6:22

1

Be Clear and Be Not Afraid: A Brief Introduction

Thomas Merton once wrote: "If you write for God you will reach many (people) and bring them joy. . . . If you write for (people)—you may make some money and you may give someone a little joy and you may make a noise in the world, for a little while. . . . If you write only for yourself you can read what you yourself have written and after ten minutes you will be so disgusted you will wish that you were dead."[1]

In preparing this manuscript, I have tried to keep these words of Merton in mind. However, again and again I could feel myself drifting away from God only to get embroiled in a concept or story that had nothing to do with the way God seemed to be calling me. Hopefully though, through prayer, personal reflection, and the comments of others I have been open enough to be guided by grace to come back to the theme upon which this book is based:

> Seeking spiritual and psychological perspective during difficult and confusing times is a process which is paradoxical in that it offers unusual opportunities to grow in our relationship with the living God *at the very time* when our faith seems the most tested and the weakest.

The extent to which what I say in this book seems to ring true is probably the best measure of how well I have succeeded in this regard.

This book was launched by an invitation to speak on the topic of spirituality and crisis at the Fourth Annual Symposium of the Isaac Taylor Institute of Psychiatry and Religion of Taylor Manor Hospital in Ellicott City, Maryland. Therefore, I am grateful to Robert McAllister, M.D., its director, and his fine staff for their invitation and encouragement.

I am also grateful to my chairperson, Mel Blanchette, S.S., Ph.D., and the faculty of the Graduate Programs in Pastoral Counseling, Loyola College in Maryland, for their enthusiasm about this project. Their interest in my work has resulted in a positive environment in which to prepare this manuscript.

To the students of the Graduate Programs in Pastoral Counseling at Loyola College in Maryland and the students in the recent courses I have taught at Washington Theological Union, Princeton Theological Seminary, and in the Graduate Department of Theology and Pastoral Ministry of St. Michael's College in Winooski, Vermont, I am also very grateful. Their strong faith commitment, constructive feedback and spontaneous reinforcement of my efforts to integrate psychology and spirituality have been good sources of inspiration for me.

Finally, I would like to thank my wife and daughter for their lessons of love and gifts of perspective. Without their presence in my life, this manuscript would not contain so much life. My wife Michaele models a deep spirituality which calls me to be all that I can be without causing me embarrassment for being where I am at the moment. And my daughter· "Shel" constantly reminds me that one of the greatest gifts persons can give each other is *respect*; she calls upon me to respect myself, respect her, and respect the lessons that I offer her and others so that what I say is how I live. To both of them, I offer my thanks and my love. I feel very lucky to have them as my family and guides, and can sense their presence in the spirit of this book.

Seeking Perspective is an outgrowth of the ideas developed in three previous books: *Availability: The Problem and the Gift* and

Living Simply in an Anxious World (both of Paulist Press), and *Self-Ministry Through Self-Understanding* (Loyola University Press). However, although this is so, this volume is meant to stand by itself as a brief work designed to explore not only how spirituality and psychology can support us in difficult times but also how, during such periods of confusion and pain, we have a unique opportunity to nurture our relationship with God and enable it to grow in surprising ways.

With this focus in mind, my goal is to present the guidance of key spiritual figures and my own relevant experiences in ways that would offer insight, practical information, and possible inspiration—especially during periods of sickness, sadness, loneliness, stress, and loss. With all of the anxiety and uncertainty in the world today, it is my aim to offer some thoughts, ideas, and encouragement which in a real (albeit small) way, may open all of us to

> see clearly, act faithfully, and appreciate deeply that we are loved by God, no matter how dark or puzzling things seem at certain times in our own lives and in the world at large.

The central tenet of this book then is: *Be clear and be not afraid, for you are loved by God.* And it is in this spirit that I offer this work to you.

Robert J. Wicks
Loyola College
Maryland

2

Spiritual Strength: A True Psychological Resource During Difficult Times

. . . a domesticated deity does not call us out to the spiritual pilgrimage. He legitimates where we already are.[1]
—Urban Holmes

Spirituality dawns when God becomes as real as the problems and joys we face each day. And as our blessings would have it, it is during the very times when losses occur and crises strike that the opportunity is especially present for God to clearly emerge as someone who is at the center of our lives, at the heart of ourselves, and on the horizon of our destiny. Until then, the *covenant* (deep relationship) we have with God may be vague, a mere backdrop, or practically forgotten. A crisis or loss can violently shake the heavy dust of denial off of our primordial and possibly childish relationship with the Lord; it can remind us of our vulnerability and dependence on the creator, and cut through the massive games of pseudo-independence we have played, thus making us cry out in anguish, shock, anxiety, impatience, and indignation at our tragedy.

When serious problems arise, patience and respectful distant pleading with God doesn't last too long. To be sure we are as patient as Job—who certainly wasn't very patient at all! In a cursory

4

examination of the text you find that he spent six chapters in patient acceptance and thirty-six chapters complaining and lamenting. And in most instances we are just like him in this regard. When God doesn't answer us as we would like, when the status quo is not returned to its original luster, we feel unfairly tested and are furious and/or doubtful about God's presence in our lives. We are angry about what we perceive as the hide-and-seek game we believe God is playing with us at a time when we feel that the divine presence is dramatically needed. As a matter of fact, if we are really being honest with ourselves, at times like these we may question whether a God exists at all. And I most assuredly include in this group of deep doubters those of us who claim to be living a life that is publicly committed to religion, pastoral care and ministry.

Henri Nouwen recognizes this tendency toward doubt about God when facing a crisis and the role "secularization" plays in it. He notes:

It is very simplistic to say that emergencies make people pay more attention to God and reawaken religious feelings. We might in fact wonder if the opposite is not more often the case. Fear and anger do not lead to God. The great pressures of our time have created much bitterness, resentment, and hatred. Many people have turned away from God and prayer since they no longer see how they can pray to a God who allows so much cruelty, so much agony, so much pain. . . . We listen to lectures affirming the importance of prayer, but we really think that our people need actions and not prayer and that prayer and praying is good when you really have nothing else to do. I wonder if under the surface of our religiosity we do not have great doubts about God's effectiveness in our world, about his interest in us—yes, even about his presence among us. I wonder if many of us are not plagued by deep, hostile feelings toward God and the idea of God without having any way to express them. I even wonder if there are many religious people for whom God is their only concern. . . . When we speak of our age as a secular age, we must first of all be willing to become aware of how deeply this secularism has entered into our own hearts and how doubt, hesitation, suspicion, anger, and even hatred corrode our relationship with God.[2]

The Response to Loss or a Crisis

When a serious crisis arises, we outwardly—or at least inwardly—argue, bargain, express our feelings of abandonment and become angry or hurt that God is allowing this to happen. We believe this to be "malevolent neglect." In response, it is no wonder that we become *noisy*. Now this style of relating to God and God's messages to us is actually not really bad. As a matter of fact, grappling with God and the words of revelation has a long respected religious tradition, particularly in Judaism.

As Rabbi Lionel Blue, the Convenor of the Religious Court of the Reform Synagogues of Great Britain, reminds us:

> Judaism is a noisy religion. The faithful are rarely silent. . . .
> Jews even study the divine law traditionally in pairs, so that they
> can argue better . . . the meaning of the name Israel [is] "one
> who struggles with God." It was not given to Jacob after quiet
> meditation, but after [a] prolonged and realistic struggle with a
> messenger of God. . . . [Jews] are not holy vegetables, bits of
> religious asparagus, [just] quietly growing upwards, complying
> with divine requirements, in a dull earthly silence.[3]

In taking the covenant seriously, Jews are quite actively involved with God. And this should be true of the committed followers of any monotheistic religion who encounter "the Other" as someone *real*, someone *true*, someone *meaningful* in their daily lives.

Expressing anguish, disillusionment and near despair with a deeply felt desire for a return of what we have lost or to a pre-crisis state is natural. As you might intimate then from my comments so far, I feel as many others do that expressing initial strong negative reactions to God during difficult times is not a problem in itself. As a matter of fact, it may be one of the signs of a faith that is real and based on an ongoing relationships with the living God.

The real difficulty in these instances arises when we don't allow ourselves or help others to move beyond anger and disillusionment with God in order to be open to the possibilities of encountering God in surprising and mysterious ways. The greatest challenge in times of crisis and loss then—as in living a faith-full or spiritually-committed life in general—is to be willing to be open to receive love in possibly new ways, from different sources, at unexpected times.

Let me illustrate by relating an interaction with a person who was plunged into an unforeseen tragic crisis. A woman and her fifty year old husband received word that he had been promoted to a key position in the Fortune 500 company in which he was employed. They were thrilled and prepared to move with their children to California. The move was coming any day and their garage was filled with boxes of household goods they had already packed.

Given all of this excitement and the fact that I had known about it because I was an acquaintance of theirs, I was shocked to find out when I came home one night what had happened earlier that evening, only days before they were due to leave. It seems that their daughter came in and had a major argument with her father. Shortly after she had stormed out, he started to feel chest pain. After a while they rushed him to the emergency room of a nearby hospital, but it was too late. He had such a massive coronary that they said in layperson's terms: "His heart just burst." They could do nothing to save him.

When his wife came to see me the next day, she was naturally very depressed and also quite angry. She looked at me directly and said: "I want you to know how angry I am at God!" I sensed from her tone, the look on her face, and the fact that she knew my work was based on religion as well as psychology, that she expected me to defend God. When I replied that if I were in her position I wouldn't be angry with God, she seemed ready to give me a real fight about it until she heard me add: "Anger wouldn't be a strong enough word to describe how I would feel. I would be violently furious at God if what happened to you had happened to me!"

Following this statement, she felt secure enough to share her wrath that this should happen to her. I helped her with this by encouraging her anger, and she let it out until, with a tired and somewhat dejected expression on her face, she mumbled that she appreciated my listening to her and got up to leave.

I stood up with her and said: "Before you go, I do want to tell you two things. First, you won't always feel as badly as you do right now. Do you believe that?" She replied: "No." I said: "That's just as I expected. If you believed this so soon after your husband's death it would be unnatural. However, what I am saying is true. I've never lied to you so I won't lie to you now. As a result, even though you don't believe it in your heart and have yet to experience it when you feel really badly, I want you to remember my words, to hold onto them with all your might."

"And secondly, I hope that you don't stay angry at God any longer than you have to." At this comment, she came to life again and jutted her jaw out at me. She gave me a look that seemed to say: "I knew all along that you were going to defend God and tell me that I shouldn't be angry with him." With this expression on her face, she challenged me in a harsh raspy voice that bespoke of sadness and anger: "Just give me one reason why you hope I won't stay angry at God after what's just happened to me!"

And I replied: "Because when we are angry with someone we put up a wall between us. And so we deprive ourselves of that person's love. And included in this love, probably the warmest love you can get in so many ways, is the love of God. I'm your friend. I know you need love during this really tough time; and, after all you've been through, I feel you deserve it. So, I hope when the time is right, you can let the wall come down and let God love you."

Upon hearing this, she looked down, cried softly, hugged and thanked me, and left. It was far from easy, but eventually she did recover from this loss and is leading a very active happy life today.

The Call

The point is that when we know we are loved and loved deeply by God, this does not mean that we won't still fight hard and furiously against injustice, sickness, poverty, death, and loss. We may also lament loudly and directly to God, asking that the burden be lifted from our shoulders. But, at the same time, we must also begin to know more deeply that we can never return to the "flesh-pots" of Egypt, or remove the necessary crosses that come with being where God wants us to be. In addition, we must never be fully satisfied living in the "jeweled casket of nostalgia." Instead, during difficult periods, we must try to begin to see that these are very special times to *remember*. Remember what? Remember the *covenant*. Remember *grace*. And remember that no matter what befalls us, God will not abandon us. Given this awareness of our close relationship with the Ultimate, we will look desperately for God in the situation—not God as we would have the creator appear and be to us, but for the God who in mysterious ways can be like a burning bush that consumes and purifies our doubts, supports our spirit and calls us to stand dependent and barefoot on holy ground where we can meet true Wisdom so that she can embrace us and open our eyes even though we may prefer to keep them anxiously shut.

A contemporary of Jesus, Rabbi Tarphon said: "The day is short, the work is great, the laborers are sluggish, the wages are high, and the Master of the house is insistent. It is not your duty to *finish* the work, but you are not free to neglect it."[4] In the gospels this theme is emphasized by Christians in terms of "the road to Jerusalem" which strongly and clearly points out the need to seek God's will and embrace God's support in all situations, even the necessarily painful ones of life.

Sometimes, somehow, we often get and give ourselves a very different message. We believe that religion will protect us from losing what we want and have in life. In such cases, religion like other good things in life (i.e. friendship, family, work . . .) gets distorted and can actually block us from experiencing God. We mistake *our* image of God and the *gifts* of God for the true undefinable God. Abraham Heschel, who comes from a long line of illustrious Hasidic rabbis, put this point forth quite poetically when he said:

> As a tree torn from the soil, as a river separated from its source, the human soul wanes when detached from what is greater than itself. . . . It is the attachment to what is spiritually superior: loyalty to a sacred person or idea, devotion to a noble friend or teacher, love for a people or for mankind, which holds our inner life together. But any ideal, human, social, or artistic, if it forms a roof over all of life, shuts us off from the light. Even the palm of one hand may bar the light of the entire sun. Indeed, we must be open to the remote in order to perceive the near. Unless we aspire to the utmost, we shrink to inferiority.[5]

And so, within the tragedy of a loss or crisis there is a real possibility to move away from the limited God we have created, and a life we may be merely existing within, to an experience of God and life that can be real and transforming in nature. Still, admitting this, and believing it at such a deep level that one can boldly act upon it are two completely different things! A life of true covenant is *simple* . . . but not *easy*.

The problems we have on a social as well as on an individual scale can be very great, and it is easy to be overwhelmed by them. We pollute the waters, sky, land and our foods. We are faced with hunger, violence and the terror of AIDS. We have been given a beautiful untamed world and we have frequently responded psychologically in a distorted "male-oriented" way by destroying much of it in an ill-fated attempt to conquer its possibilities. Rarely are we "psychologically-female" in our orientation to the world; by that I mean that too infrequently do we *sit with* our gifts from God and *affiliate* with the world in a way in which the plants that grow, the fish that swim the seas, and the animals that populate the earth can flourish *with* us.

Consequently, the problems we have, seem great on both a social and an individual level. Unfortunately for us God frequently seems so absent, so unreal in these troubled days. If we are authentic in times as these we may ask ourselves and our religion again and again: "What possibilities can faith and spirituality really offer us as resources during a time of crisis?"

Well, this is, I think, where true prayer and a deep, thoroughly-challenging sense of spirituality come in and are given the opportunity to surprise us, move us to a new level of personal integration and, of course, lead to essential social action. One of my favorite quotes is from Jim Fenhagen who is the dean of General Theological Seminary in New York and the author of *Invitation to Holiness*. He says: "People live cautiously because they pray cautiously."[6]

In a time of crisis or loss when our lament for a return of the status quo fails, a natural inclination is to be conservative and hesitant in our belief because the results we want, in the way we want them, when we want them, don't seem very visible. As a result, it doesn't seem sensible to believe. However, we must try *not* to be sensible as the world might have us be in this regard, because at times like these true prayer throws caution to the wind and lets us be open in a way that our faith and spirituality can form a new basis for psychological awareness and growth. And this is exactly what we need to happen—especially during difficult times!

FAITH AND SPIRITUALITY AS PSYCHOLOGICAL RESOURCES IN TIMES OF CRISIS AND LOSS

Much has been written on the integration of psychology and spirituality. Still more has been written on how psychology can aid in the development of a mature faith. However, with the exception of Gerald May[7] and several others, little has been explicitly written on *how spirituality can inform and support good psychology* rather than the other way round. Yet this is exactly what I am referring to here. And so, what I would like to focus on at this point is the role that faith, prayer and spirituality can play as possible psychological resources in times of crisis and loss. The two themes I would like to discuss here to illustrate this belief in the psychological value of a sound spirituality and a strong faith during troubled times are: (1) the value of faith as a force which can fight despair and cynicism and transform doubt into something positive—i.e. a new opening to a greater sense of God and life; (2) the role of having a sound spirituality when a crisis causes stress on self-esteem and encourages a distorted sense of self-awareness.

Faith vs. Cynicism and Despairing Doubt

Without faith and the deep sense of covenant that comes with it, a loss can often set the stage for cynicism and a despairing sense of doubt that digs a deep hole from which one's human enthusiasm may never be able to fully emerge again. This is especially so in the case of the young. As Maya Angelou, poet and author of the stirring autobiography *I Know Why the Caged Bird Sings*, aptly notes: "There is nothing so tragic as a young cynic. For the young cynic is going from knowing nothing to believing nothing."[8]

People of faith, the spiritually committed, can often feel the love *of* God, and their own love *for* God, lying just below the surface of their psyches. They live their lives with a pre-conscious awareness of God's incarnational love and it is reinforced on a daily basis by an almost pre-logical form of communication with the presence of God in the world. This daily contact with God is necessary to set the stage for those dramatic periods in our lives which will lift up and befall all of us.

The theologian Karl Rahner addresses this theme in the following way:

We cannot assert that someone who is well behaved, devout, and virtuous in ordinary life, is also already certain of surviving the great situations where it is a question of life or death. The grace of such endurance is a grace that no one can merit by good behavior in ordinary life. But ordinary life is indeed the way in which we must remain ready for the decisive situations; it can be the way in which God wants to give us the very grace—which we cannot demand—of surviving the great hours of our life. We must be faithful in little things in order to be permitted to hope that God in his grace will also send us faithfulness in great things.[9]

And once again, to turn to the words of Rabbi Heschel who deals with this theme in a slightly different way:

Whatever the pious [person] does is linked to the divine; each smallest trifle is tangential to [God's] course. In breathing he uses [God's] force; in thinking he wields [God's] power. He moves always under the unseen canopy of remembrance, and the wonderful weight of the name of God rests steadily on his mind. The word of God is as vital to him as air or food. He is never alone, never companionless, for God is within reach of his heart. . . . The pious [person] needs no miraculous communication to make him aware of God's presence. . . . His awareness may be overlaid momentarily or concealed by some violent shift in consciousness, but it never fades away.[10]

In other words, persons of faith, at some level, are ready for crises, in the same way that they are ready for *all* daily occurrences, to open up new doors.

So, although a crisis is just as painful for the spiritual person as it is for one who has little or no conscious faith, in the faith-full individual the doubt does not point only to despair but—amidst the pain—to new hopes built on a renewed faith and a new dynamic image of God. As a matter of fact, *the amount of real trust we have*

*in God is sometimes best measured by the depth of the doubt and
the seriousness of the questions with which we are willing to live.*

Rather than removing the doubts, prayer may instead help us
more and more to see the truth and hold onto the possible as well as
the probable without pain. Serious believers are critical thinkers.
When a crisis dawns and threatens the very core of their identity
and their faith, they are willing to continue to respond and search—
not because of religion (which in many cases loses its way because
of an obsession over trivialities), but because of their belief in the
living God and a desire to live with that God now in some new way,
rather than to merely exist.

Once a great master told a story to his disciples, and it was on
the theme of life:

> He told of meeting a pilot who flew laborers from China into
> Burma during World War II to work on jungle roads. The
> flight was long and boring, so the laborers would take to gam-
> bling. Since they had no money to gamble with, they gambled
> with their lives—the loser jumped out of the plane without a
> parachute!
>   "How terrible!" said the horrified disciples.
>   "True," said the Master. "But it made the game
> exciting."[11]

The point the master was obviously making was: "You never live so
fully as when you gamble with your lives."[12]

When something terrible happens it awakens us to life and the
reality of our present limits and eventual death in a way that success,
comfort and prosperity never could. True prayer can serve as a
counterbalance in such instances to the insulating and denying
forces of a world which encourages us to think otherwise or, more
accurately, not to think at all. Spiritual persons ultimately have the
opportunity to meet tragedy in a different way because they meet
life in general in a different way. By wrapping themselves in silence,
solitude, and gratitude, they open their hearts in a contemplative

way again and again to perspective and simplicity. They are able to hear God in a world of sorrows, joys, uncertainties, and limits because the lost art of listening, really listening to the universe, can be gracefully recovered again and again in the sabbath experience of silence and solitude.

What I am speaking about here is not pietistical passivity. I am speaking about the willingness to accept life unconditionally and to fathom its possibilities within the limits of failure, sinfulness, and death.

A practical theme of the psychiatrist William Glasser was that in life we must learn to recognize the givens, understand the givens, accept the givens and live within the givens.[13] Recognition . . . understanding . . . acceptance . . . and a willingness to live within the givens—that's what we need. Yet, faith, prayer and spirituality can determine in a significant way *how* we will do this. As resignation moves toward acceptance, real healing and crisis resolution takes place. A strong faith offers the environment where this can occur and leads to greater integration and maturity—no matter what the problem.

A case in point is the way persons who have been diagnosed with AIDS lead their lives. After moving through all of the initial stages one naturally goes through after hearing that he or she has AIDS, there is a crossroads. One path leads to denial and despair . . . the other to holiness. Spiritually attuned persons who have AIDS are in a good position to be firmly covenantal at such a crisis point. They have the possibility to be truly awake to a more meaningful relationship with self, others and God than ever before; moreover, this enlightenment can pervade the rest of their lives. This doesn't mean that these persons would not still wish that a cure could be found in time to save them; also, periodic negativity in the form of depression, anxiety and anger might still stir within them, for this is natural and human—we must remember that holiness and perfection are not synonymous. However, during this terrible tragic period in their lives, if their faith is strong, they are in a special position to experience life more deeply and richly than many of us who are "doomed" to live a long life of compulsive existence. Those of us who have encountered such persons know what I mean.

Now, let me present you with a contrast to illustrate my point. Most of my private practice is conducted with therapists and persons in active ministry. Recently a psychologist whose life was out of control consulted me. He reminded me of a person completely lost in the center of the city, desperately trying to find a route to his home in the suburbs but terribly stymied because he had a blindfold over his eyes. My intervention with him was metaphorically akin to telling him how to take the blindfold off so he could formulate a plan to free himself from his addiction to achieving "success"—as he had envisioned it up to this point. Yet, instead of responding affirmatively to my suggestion his initial response to me essentially was: "I don't have the time to take off my blindfold; can't you see I'm too busy trying to find my way home?"

Tell me, at that moment who was more alive—the person of faith with AIDS or this psychologist? Although much of the world may applaud the driven psychologist for his achievement, the young spiritually attuned AIDS person is in constant meaningful dialogue with himself, others, and God; he is trying to live every moment of his life rather than run from it under the disguise of being productive. And, by the same token, what a wonderful way for this young "sick" person to live out what's left of his life . . . even if it is to be brief and more so because this is seen as something negative in a world where longevity is often valued much more than wisdom.

I guess the lesson is that perspective must be fought for each day if we are to maintain an awareness of what's really important without having to be awakened again and again by a crisis or loss. The choice is up to us, and a strong faith and spirituality which allows a quiet period each day to cut through the compulsive lies of life and helps us to breathe in the truth of knowing what really matters certainly can help in this regard.

Spiritual and psychological growth occurs only when insight encourages both our hearts and our minds to give up the "advantage" of staying the same in order to opt for something that is greater yet unknown. Yet, one of the greatest human paradoxes is that we seem to complain the most about a lack of spiritual passion in our lives at the very time when we are willing to gamble the least. Still, it is hard to have vision if we are busy holding on tightly to the present, continue to be preoccupied with the past, or fail to be open to a future that may dash the status quo against the rocks of the beachhead of the "kindom" of God. However, this is the very place that people of faith are being called to during a crisis. How they respond will determine whether their faith will fall by the side or whether it will serve as a new platform which will help them stand on their own two feet supported *only by their covenant with God.*

Basil Pennington, in his book of reflections on Thomas Merton, treats this theme:

> In his last talk, the one given at the Pan-Asian Monastic Conference in Bangkok, Merton related a story about Chogyam Trungpa Rimpoche. At the critical moment when Rimpoche had to make his decision about leaving Tibet (after a military/ political "crackdown" by the Chinese), he found himself isolated in a mountain hut. He did not know what to do. So he sent to a neighboring abbot friend, saying, "What do we do?" The answer came back: "From now on, Brother, everybody stands on his own two feet." Tom commented that that was an extremely important statement. We all do need some external supports and structures to grow . . . yet true freedom demands that we be free even from the communities and the structures that support us. Ultimately there is no friend who can fully understand us, who can walk with us all the way. We must go forward and walk on our own in response to who we are and who we are called to be in God.[14]

Pennington also pointed out:

> When [Thomas Merton] was preparing an article on the
> Georgian letters of Boris Pasternak, he spoke to the community
> at Gethsemani about them. He pointed out and commented at
> length on a particular statement in the last of the letters written
> shortly before Pasternak's death (in which he said): "Every-
> where in the world one has to pay for the right to live on one's
> naked spiritual reserves."[15]

Pennington believes as Merton does that the cost is great to
come to this point of complete freedom and that Merton was willing
to pay the price. The question is: Are we? I think that people with
deep faith are. And during periods of crisis and loss, it is this very
deep faith, this covenant with God, which helps them deal with
doubt and work through cynicism. In addition, it sets the stage for
them to increase self-awareness and self-esteem at the very time
when the movement of a crisis is trying to make them crumble.

A CRISIS, SELF-ESTEEM, AND SPIRITUALITY

A crisis can lead to a point where the usual sources of self-
esteem are eroded and one is left naked and vulnerable. When we
are in the midst of a crisis, we certainly don't see a clear way out.
We feel like the deep-sea diver who had scarcely reached the ocean
floor when a message which left him in a dilemma came from the
surface. It said: "Come up quickly . . . the ship is sinking!"
        We are all loyal to at least one negative view of ourselves. It is
the deep negative belief that cognitive therapists speak about or the
driving unconscious force from early in life that the dynamically-
oriented psychotherapists focus on in their work. Depression often
occurs when we have forgotten to love the presence of God in all
living things—including, maybe especially, in ourselves.

A spirituality that recognizes we are always special in the eyes of God and that the so-called "specialness-in-the-eyes-of-the-world" is non-existent, or at best fleeting, helps us to appreciate what a crisis can teach us. Robert Frost once made the comment: "Education is the ability to listen to almost anything without losing your temper or your self-confidence."

We are very tied to our image, and often we don't even know it or for that matter appreciate how temporary and illusory trying to hold onto or put faith in our image can be. I remember a small event that happened several years ago which I try to recall anytime I feel myself losing perspective with respect to my own image.

I had been asked by a colleague to give a workshop at a government installation for Veterans' Administration employees. After a longer drive than I had expected, I arrived at the base feeling a bit annoyed. But all of my annoyance lifted and was replaced by pride when I noticed a large marquee by the front gate which bore the following message in three-foot letters: WELCOME DR. ROBERT WICKS! I thought to myself: "Oh, how I wish I had a camera so I could take a picture of this for my *mother*." (Never mind my wife; I regressed all the way back into childhood!) Then I drove over to a large theater which looked as though it could hold thousands. As I got out and walked toward the large hall, I thought to myself: "I didn't realize how famous I was; this important address to such a large group could be my finest hour." Then when I got inside, there were only twelve people waiting for me to speak. I guess God was trying to keep me and my ego in conversation!

Self-awareness and healthy self-love go hand in hand. If anything, spiritual self-awareness is really a religious way of viewing self-confidence because it is a self-confidence *not* built on lies we have told ourselves, but on an appreciation of the footprints of God in our own personality and an understanding of how we often block those footprints from becoming clear to ourselves and others.

Sartre once claimed that "to live well is difficult and yet possible." For the person of faith this becomes truly possible in a crisis through the reception of God's grace. The fascinating theologian Rudolf Bultmann once noted:

> God's grace is to [a person's] grace in such a thoroughgoing sense that it supports the whole of [a person's] existence, and can only be conceived of as grace by those who surrender their whole existence and let themselves fall into the unfathomable dizzy depths without seeking for something to hold on to.[16]

Several years ago something happened to me that made Bultmann's point painfully clear to me. I was asked to do a series of lectures for a group of people who had very low morale. This request was not surprising in itself because I am often requested to go into difficult situations and to present the truth in a way that new possibilities and hopes can spring from the psychological and spiritual ashes of hurt feelings, discarded religious structures, and the stress which expectations to live one's individual and community life in new ways naturally brings with it.

The surprising thing for me was that nothing seemed to work. Not only did the group seem to hate me before I arrived, but they also appeared to hold onto this feeling during the period that I was working with them. The result was that I began to feel insecure, anxious, somewhat depressed and angry. And this was reflected in my prayer life as well.

In my time spent alone with God I asked to be relieved of the situation. (At some level, I think I also wished I could pray an Old Testament prayer: "Smite all of these people, their families, friends . . . including their children!" However, I knew God would say: "We don't do that anymore!")

The response that I seemed to receive to my prayers didn't really appear to be an answer at the time. The sense I got in prayer was that God was asking me whether I thought I had discerned properly that coming to this situation was in fact God's will and not my desire to perform in a spectacular fashion. I responded in prayer affirmatively. Then God seemed to say to me: "Then why are all of these complaints relevant? People did terrible things to me when I obeyed my Father, and many years ago I also told you that on occasion they would do the same, if not worse, to you if you chose to pick up your cross, be obedient and follow me."

What could I say after sensing this response from God? I realized that I had become so used to people appreciating my ministry of teaching that when the going got rough, as Jesus had warned me might happen long ago, I had a hard time with it. I was more concerned with my image than in simply being obedient to the call to serve and be in solidarity with these troubled and pressured people.

One of the positive outcomes of all of this, however, was that I think I care a little less now about my image and can spend more of my energy seeing whether I am responding to God as I am being called each day or following my anxious ego's continuous demand to inflate or protect itself. So, in the case of a person of faith, while a crisis may be just as painful, it can, as Rabbi Kushner pointed out in his famous book *When Bad Things Happen to Good People*, lead to growth rather than bitterness. The guidance comes from being in touch with God. And the choice is usually up to us whether we will avail ourselves of such help. Maybe that is why small and large difficulties in life are the painful "crossroads" in which our faith can either atrophy or grow dramatically.

PRAYER, SPIRITUALITY AND FAITH— FOUNDATION DURING TIMES OF CRISIS AND LOSS

And so, as can be surmised from my comments thus far, I believe that prayer, spirituality and faith can be strong foundations during times of crisis and loss. A living faith can give real life when all possibilities seem dead.

A number of years ago, J.P. Dubois-Dumee reflected on the

movement in many people's lives toward a spiritual renewal—in particular a renewal of prayer. He felt that when one looks at the desire to make one's faith come alive through prayer and attention to one's faith, one can detect among other things:

a need for permanence in a civilization of transience;

a need for the Absolute when all else has become relative;

a need for silence in the midst of noise;

a need for gratuitousness in the face of unbelievable greed;

a need for poverty amid the flaunting of wealth;

a need for contemplation in a century of action, for without contemplation, action risks becoming mere agitation;

a need for communication in a universe content with entertainment and sensationalism;

a need for peace amid today's universal outbursts of violence;

a need for quality to counterbalance the increasingly prevalent response to quantity;

a need for humility to counteract the arrogance of power and science;

a need for human warmth when everything is being rationalized or computerized;

a need to belong to a small group rather than to be part of a crowd;

a need for slowness to compensate the present eagerness for speed;

a need for truth when the real meaning of words is distorted in political speeches and sometimes even in religious discourses;

a need for transparency when everything seems opaque. Yes, a need for the interior life. . . .[17]

Albert Schweitzer, a profound activist for good, would have probably agreed with this need. He saw so much sickness, death, poverty, and tragedy. He did so much to alleviate the pain of others. Yet, he also had a foundation of faith that kept him going. But more than that, he saw the foundation of faith as a way to meet social crises and losses as well. Once he said: "One truth stands firm. All that happens in world history rests on something spiritual. If the spiritual is strong, it creates world history. If it is weak, world history suffers."

A covenant of love with God makes it possible to remember healthy self-love when a crisis would normally lead to a loss of self-confidence. A covenant of love with God also makes it possible during times of tragedy to be able to receive love from others so we can return it—at a time when normally it would seem that we should only be self-involved. One need only talk to the medical staff who cared for Hubert Humphrey during his last days to see a clear example of this; they remember less about his needs as a patient and more about his love now that he is gone—he left a legacy of love for them in the way he met his last days fully and generatively.

Teilhard de Chardin once wrote: "The day will come when, after mastering the ether, the winds, the tides, gravity, we shall master the energies of love for God. And then, for the second time in the history of the world, [people] will have made fire [their] servant."[18] This is the "fire" of faith I have been emphasizing here. This is the fire which can burn no matter what darkness comes. And like the ever-present hot pot of tea the Irish have warming on their stoves to help guard against the chill of a cold rainy winter afternoon, a strong faith stands by constantly, although quietly at times, waiting to warm us down deep so we can *remember*.

Remember what? Remember the *covenant*. Remember *grace*. And remember that the sun is not gone forever and the clouds are not permanent . . . only the presence of God is eternal.

3

Enemies of Spiritual and Psychological Perspective

"Why is everyone here so happy except me?"

"Because they have learned to see goodness and beauty everywhere," said the Master.

"Why don't I see goodness and beauty everywhere?"

"Because you cannot see outside of you what you fail to see inside."

———————————— ○○○ ————————————

"How shall I get liberation?"

"Find out who has bound you," said the Master.

The disciple returned after a week and said, "No one has bound me."

"Then why ask to be liberated?"

That was a moment of Enlightenment for the disciple, who suddenly became free.

———————————— ○○○ ————————————

To a disciple who complained of his limitations the Master said, "You are limited indeed. But have you noticed you can do things today that you would have thought impossible fifteen years ago? What changed?"

"My talents changed."

"No. You changed."
"Isn't that the same thing?"
"No. You are what you think you are. When your
thinking changed, you changed."
—Three stories told by Anthony de Mello[1]

In 1972, a little over a week before the great Rabbi Abraham Heschel died, he was asked by an interviewer for NBC-TV if he had a message for today's youth. Rather than being put off by such a broad and challenging question, he nodded affirmatively and said: "Remember, that there is meaning beyond absurdity. Know that every deed counts, that every word is power . . . above all, remember that you must build your life as if it were a work of art."[2]

His words to the young then should still be a calling cry to both the young and mature of our day as well. However, knowing a worthy goal such as this, and being able to fulfill it on a daily basis, are two radically different things. There are many blocks to spiritual and psychological perspective which must be unmasked and dealt with every day. Otherwise, the gift of perspective which God offers anew each day will remain unwrapped and unused and we will be beleaguered by unnecessary worries, doubts, and anxieties. The result: confusion instead of clarity, passivity in lieu of passion, and withdrawal in place of solidarity with others. In such instances, rather than building our life as if it were a work of art, we will feel wrecked in emotions which will tell us we are lost, overwhelmed, and unsettled.

Both a Feminine and Masculine Call

For *all* of us, the call to spiritual and psychological perspective is both a feminine and masculine one. From a "masculine orientation" we have traditionally been called psychologically to *separate*, *individuate* and be *mature* adults according to the theme of 1 Corinthians 12 which calls us to discover and prize the uniqueness we have to contribute to the world. The spiritual goal, from such a vantage point then, is *obedience* to God's call to be all that we can be as persons made in the image and likeness of God; at its core it is a cognitive call to try to think, perceive, and understand who God wants us to be and what the Lord wants us to do in life.

However, this is not possible unless we also heed the "feminine" call to *psychological affiliation* and *spiritual solidarity*. We can't go to God alone; if and when we try, the dangers are great. Withdrawal and isolation can easily masquerade as solidarity with God; religious elitism can often be touted and supported as if it were real piety; and an absence of affect, which can leave us feeling emotionally sterile, may be inappropriately seen positively as true "detachment" or "ascesis" which it never is.

So, the call to perspective is both a call to be mature and in community. It is a call to forsake both passivity and willfulness in our movement toward personal and communal development. And to respond to this simple but difficult call, we must do all in our power to flow with the grace of God by uncovering and dealing with the enemies of perspective which assail us at every turn. Three of the major ones I would like to present here are:

- Self-esteem problems;
- Anxieties due to an inordinate fear of failure, doubt, and change;
- A pollution of our spirit due to negativity.

Self-Esteem Problems

Some people are fully human—so much so that when we are with them we feel very peaceful, accepted . . . it is all right for us to be ourselves.

In their presence we seem to breathe more easily, speak more freely, and smile more naturally. It is as if we didn't age during the time we were with them because we felt too relaxed to wear out—even a little.

Then after leaving them we feel some regret. To be with them again would be great. Even better! To be more like them ourselves, to be real, to be open, to be free to be ourselves in all types of situations with all kinds of people, wouldn't that be just wonderful! Not only would this be a personally peaceful way of life, it would be pure gift for others because *one of the greatest things we can do for others is to learn to "like" ourselves.* (I don't mean "love" ourselves —that's too philosophical. I mean "like" ourselves—"get a kick" out of ourselves!)

The reason why this type of attitude would be helpful to others rather than being merely narcissistic is clear. People with solid self-esteem are less defensive, better able to deal with the pain and negativity of others, as well as being in a good position to inspire true hope in others.

People who know themselves and are at peace with themselves always have something to share, no matter how difficult the situation turns out to be. They are alive, and those who encounter them enjoy the possibility of living more clear and meaningful lives because of the gentle open space they offer them. (This is the general principle behind such processes as psychotherapy and spiritual direction/guidance.)

People who are in touch with their own gifts, are grateful to God for them, and seek to nurture them, are like oases for the worried, anxious, poor, depressed and oppressed of the world. They are a place of refuge. In some cases, for some reason, persons like this seem to do it naturally. And so, they may not be conscious of being this way themselves or be very noticeable to others. In addition, age is not a factor; people like this thrive and encourage others at each level of human development.

I remember being "in love" in junior high school. Her name was Pam. She was marvelous. There was only one problem: I couldn't tell anyone because she wasn't the type one was allowed to fall head over heels in love with. In adolescence, one's "loves" are like mirrors. They have to look a certain way because the important thing is how you look standing next to them. Now Pam was attractive to me but she didn't look the part as dictated by the norm informally set out by my friends (not tall enough or the right color hair), so I tried to hide my feelings for fear of being ostracized—a terrible thing for me at fifteen!

Yet, in my heart I liked her in spite of it all and occasionally it showed. This resulted in a few close calls with respect to my friends. However, it wasn't until just a few years ago when I was reminiscing about school that I remembered this part of my life and finally realized why I liked Pam so much. It was because she liked, really liked herself. Not in a narcissistic way, but almost in a fun way. She "got a kick" out of Pam. She enjoyed being herself and being spontaneous with others. She seemed to like who she was and who she was becoming. This provided a lift for me and I'm sure for others who knew her then and probably now as well.

This lesson was brought closer to home several years ago when I was teaching at a local Franciscan college. Its president—who was also a psychologist—was resigning to take a sabbatical. We were sitting in her office and saying our goodbyes. I told her that her greatest gift to me was her ability to forgive. Since sometimes I was impetuous, in my intensity and involvement I had occasionally said and done things which were somewhat painful for her. Yet, although we had had our differences, she had repeatedly "wiped the slate clean," and for this I told her I was very grateful.

In response, she said that she wanted to share with me what she felt was one of my greatest gifts. She said: "No matter how many things you have written, no matter how much you've accomplished or become well known in certain circles, you have never lost your childlike nature with respect to yourself. You seem always to be surprised and enjoy the new things you find out about yourself." And what she said stuck with me because, although it may not sound like much, it was one of the most important compliments I had ever received.

This comment is a benchmark statement for me with respect to mental health and spiritual wisdom. To be unrelentingly open with respect to oneself is the lifelong goal of self-knowledge and self-esteem. I believe that from a psychological perspective one of the most serious sins is to ignore, deny, or worship our own personalities rather than to prize them, find out all about them, and seek to express them naturally and freely with a sense of *mitzvah* (giving and expecting nothing in return). To have a sense of awe about the presence of God everywhere, including (maybe especially) oneself, changes the way one leads one's life.

Anxieties Due to an Inordinate Fear of Failure, Doubt, and Change

Perspective is an essential key to psychological and spiritual wholeness. If our attitude is healthy and our spirit sound, then whom shall we fear? In common parlance, how long must we worry unnecessarily? Why should we be upset for longer than is normal when we face the difficulties of daily life?

Matthew Fox suggests that we replace the word "faith" in the scriptures with the word "trust." In such a scenario, failure, doubt, and change will lead us to a greater rather than lesser faith. An attitude built on trust (in other words, an attitude of hope built on a living faith) can change how we see and experience everything— including even normally defeating events. In Christ's words: "If therefore your eye is good, your whole body will be full of light" (Mt 6:22).

Failure can awaken us to life in a much more dramatic way than success ever could. After all, embarrassment and awkwardness are the handles that God's redemptive grace holds onto. When failure shakes us, it is really shaking our false images not our true selves. God doesn't call us to be successful (that's a secular command). God simply calls us to respond. And knowing this lesson of grace and God's gratuitousness is essential if we wish to be caring Christians. The more we are involved in God's work, and the bigger our world of interactions becomes, the more we are apt to make mistakes and have the natural inclination to pull back.

And yet, even if we succumb to our anxieties and try to withdraw, we won't feel peace; withdrawal offers no guarantee of security. As the humorist Robert Benchley wryly noted: "My only solution for the problem of habitual accidents . . . is for everybody to stay in bed all day. Even then, there is always the chance that you will fall out."

Fear of doubt is another enemy of spiritual and psychological perspective. Former secretary of state John Foster Dulles once said: "If you are scared to go to the brink, you are lost." The same can be said of faith. Faith that doesn't include risk is often a sham.

Although we can encounter God everywhere, one of the best places to meet the Lord is *in the void*. In stillness, in silence, in solitude, we become frightened. We look either for something to hold onto or for something to fill us. We may turn to prayer, seeking structure, results, or a proven way. But such prayer is actually a flight from the void rather than a contemplative acceptance of it. This goes counter to the call to let go, "simply" be ourselves, and meet God in a real, unique relationship. As Thomas Merton says: "Looking for God is like seeking a path in a field of snow; if there is no path and you are looking for one, walk across it and there is your path."[3]

The void challenges us, despite our distractions, to see things and God as they are. Our depressive, anxious, stressful feelings are sometimes the result of our putting our psychological and spiritual "hands" around something less than God. Instead of just sitting in silence and solitude with God, facing our boredom, lack of control, loneliness, and inner fragmentation, our prayer tends to become mechanical. In our lives too, we try to fill the void with addictions:

to work, food, drugs, alcohol, worry, money, power, order, the church . . . yes, even prayer.

In one of my trips outside of the United States I came face to face with this issue. Having flown for hours, I was picked up at the airport and deposited at a hotel. After unpacking, I sat on the edge of the bed and looked around the room. It was clean and sparse. After a few minutes I began to feel lonely and empty. I even thought: "What if I died here; no one would really know me or feel awful about it." When I experienced this depressive thinking, my first inclination as a good psychologist was to simply tell myself that this was depressive thinking and to distract myself by calling or writing someone, or by reading one of the books I had brought with me.

But then I realized that although this would temporarily lift the depression I was experiencing, it would do little for me in the long run. I would not be dealing with the underlying cause for my loneliness and dark thoughts. When I would be in a situation like this again, I would be lonely again. Nothing would have changed. So, instead I sat with, and in, the void. But this time I was alone with my thoughts and with God.

At first my situation seemed to get worse. I began to see my own finitude, appreciate the ugly truths about myself, and feel helpless that I had no real answers to the big questions in the world. I began to get in touch with my feelings of alienation and anxiety about being a stranger, among people whom I didn't know and who didn't know me. Finally, after a while, I had the strange feeling that it would be all right. By facing my own lies about myself, my inability to control things, my sense of being a charlatan *before a loving God*, I could begin to be free. I could be free to accept God's love and to embrace this painful but liberating truth: in the eyes of the world I shall never be seen as special for any length of time, yet in the eyes of the Lord I am always special.

This lesson of grace helped me to be more open to myself and the new people I met on this trip. I greeted them as unknown friends instead of frightening strangers. I also began to see the danger of the "spiritual romanticism" that remains present even at times when I profess to be interested in being in real relationship with God. This tendency toward spiritual romanticism is something we would rather forget. Let me change that: it is something I frequently would like to forget. It is not surprising then that James Finley says the following about Thomas Merton to serve as a reminder to us about this danger:

> Merton's life was not a romantic adventure. . . . He woke before dawn with a mind "not totally reconciled to being out of bed." He ate, worked walked in the woods and prayed. In the winter he was cold and in the summer he was hot. And that is the true self. It is the self that is nobody, that is ordinary and poor. It is this ordinary self that is extraordinary for it is this ordinary self one with the moment, one with the concrete reality of everyday life, that is the self God creates, the poor self made rich in the poverty of the cross.[4]

An inordinate fear of change is another block to perspective. Change can break through comfortable familiarity and uncover prejudice. Jesus called for a new loyalty that would put God above others, no matter who they are in our lives (Mt 11:37). Too often we form God in our own image rather than being open to a growing presence of God in us and the world at large. It's no wonder then that in the early fourteenth century, Meister Eckhart noted: "I pray to God to free me of God, for God's sake," and that Celie, the central character in the novel *The Color Purple*, is told "You can't see anything at all until you get man off your eyeball."[5] It is at this point in the story that Celie is handcuffed by her image of God as an old, uncaring, white male with whom she can't relate, rather than seeing God as the *living* God who calls her to be in *relationship*. This is what we call "spirituality."

Change often unmasks our delusions, the scenarios we set up in which God protects us in our comfortability. In the events that occur on the road to Emmaus (Lk 24), it is this theme which comes through. We begin to recognize that the spiritual journey, if we may call it that, is a journey of unlearning. In the spirit of John of the Cross in his *Ascent of Mount Carmel*, we recognize the value of change in our journey to God: "The more darkness it causes, the greater light it gives." From this vantage point, confusion isn't bad if it brings with it greater concern and increases our willingness to learn what God may be teaching us and where God may be leading us.

Negativity

Another enemy of psychological and spiritual perspective is the negativity that infects us due to the great frustration and sadness we encounter in the world. In being a caring parent, family member, friend, co-worker, or minister, it is impossible for us not to be affected by the pain and helplessness of others.

Several years ago I remember returning home after a day of seeing patients in my private practice. When I came in, my wife Michaele asked me how my day was. In response I was ready to say, "Fine" (which is what most of us say almost automatically no matter how things really are). But I was overcome with such a deep sense of sadness that I said, "Terrible." She replied by asking: "Why, what happened?" Looking at her, I sat down on the kitchen chair without taking off my raincoat. Then as I have taught others, I reviewed the day to see what had happened, what I had blown out of proportion, what negative belief I was allowing to get hold of me.

And then I recognized what it was. It was not one specific event, it was a series of almost unrecognized ones. It wasn't some great problem I had to deal with that day. Instead, as I sat there reflecting, I began to see that over the past weeks, without realizing it, I had begun to absorb people's anxieties, sadness, helplessness, and hopelessness until I could no longer continue to help them. The abuse, loneliness, financial and marital difficulties, sexual addictions, interpersonal rebuffs, angers, and hardships had all been taken in by me and I felt slowly defeated by them. I could now fully appreciate what a woman once shared with me in a reflection paper: "I am amazed that so much sadness could fit into my body."

I think that no matter how we take care of ourselves, such instances will overtake us. Paradoxically, they can be graced moments. If we let them, they can bring us back to the recognition that we are called neither to win nor to abandon the fight to rid the world of darkness. We are not the ones called to effect a cure. We are "only" called to be present and to do what we can. At times like these, we must try to deal with our own "negative grandiosity." We must seek to deflate our "savior complex," our desire to be spectacular, to have an impact. We must recognize our temptation to "go it alone," and our own negative thinking when we fail. We must also be aware of what good things are taking place in the world, our world, and to sit with our negativity and desires to control things. In a gentle way we must begin to see what can be learned from the kind of thinking which has produced such distressful feelings.

Often we try either to run away from our own feelings of despair or to conquer them. We need to stay with them—in Jungian terms, to make friends with our "shadow"—to see what can come out of the darkness for us. At the very least, we will begin to see how we have relied too much on ourselves and that, in focusing on the problems of the world, *we have forgotten to see what is right in it*. A short story by a Vietnamese Zen Roshi points this out. He said: "During the [Vietnam] war, we were so busy helping the wounded that we sometimes forgot to smell the flowers. Night has a very pleasant smell [in Vietnam], especially in the country. But we would forget to pay attention to the smell of mint, coriander, thyme, and sage."[6]

Another point to recognize in this area is that one of the surest ways to let negativity get hold of us is *not to take care of ourselves*.

One of the things that I try to do is to get enough rest, food and exercise and have enough supportive people in my life. Then when people come to me to hear a presentation or ask for some advice, I am healthy enough to be really available to them. I want them to feel that they can drop anything on me without having to worry about me, that they can even be angry, contentious or in a panic and I will be free enough to help. Still, this attitude is not really a popular one, especially in Christian circles. There is a great call for people who are involved to look overworked and be overburdened. When you don't fit into this category, people are thrown off by it.

Once I was on a trip out of the United States to teach for a week. Afterward I planned to teach in Vermont for several weeks. Knowing this, one person said to me: "You poor thing, you really are overworked." Puzzled, I responded, "I'm not sure what you mean." She went on to explain that she thought I must be exhausted from teaching every day for a week in her country. To this I responded that I was really enjoying myself; the challenge was a good one. Not to be undone by this, she said "But you will be going back to teach after this, won't you?" I answered: "Yes, but I will have a week off between here and my teaching in Vermont." Still, she pressed on with her point: "But after teaching there for three weeks, you'll certainly be exhausted." I responded to this as well by pointing out that I would have weekends off in Vermont and was taking a week at Martha's Vineyard after that as my official vacation. This seemed to stop her, but after a short pause her attitude seemed to completely shift in the other direction, and her eyes seemed to now say: "My, but you take a lot of time off!" I guess there's not much room in "church circles" for people who shun Christian masochism.

Another aspect of taking care of ourselves is to *have supportive people in our lives.* A number of these have to take empathic, teaching roles, but certainly among them are those loyal people who will let us know in no uncertain terms that they are behind us.

In being committed Christians we will always have the proph-

ets in our lives who will keep us on the track. Not to have such
people to call us to be all that we can be and to challenge us when
we stray from the path is very dangerous. But I think it is almost
equally dangerous not to have very sympathetic people—real
cheerleaders—in our lives who encourage us fully at every turn. I
always tease people, particularly those in ministry, that they need
the kind of individuals who, in response to our complaints about
others, give us so much support that we almost feel guilty. And
when we express some annoyance at a person or persons, they say
something like: "You are *totally* right and they are *totally* wrong. As
a matter of fact, I am getting on my knees this very moment to pray
for their early happy death!"

Behind my silly musings there is a serious point: we can't go it
alone. We need a balance of support. We need criticism and feedback as much as we need encouragement and acceptance. Without
such a balance, we face the twin challenges of either going on our
own "Christian safari," thinking we are doing God's will, of being
crushed under the crosses of commitment that can only be held up
when we are part of a supportive community of believers. As Henri
Nouwen recognizes: "We can take a lot of physical and even mental pain when we know that it truly makes us a part of the life we live
together in the world. But when we feel cut off from the human
family, we quickly lose heart."[7]

A *Life of Perspective . . . A Simple Life of Possibilities*

Maxim Gorky, in his autobiography, quoted his grandfather:
" 'In my days dresses were far richer and finer than they are today,'
he would say. 'They spent more on dresses then, but lived more
simply, peacefully.' "[8] I feel this quote is reflective of what the
spiritual life is all about. The spiritual life is not so much filling
oneself with love or special reinforcing positive experiences but
instead allowing the love we already have to blossom. With such an
attitude inconsequential concerns lose their power so the possibili-

ties of God can surface. The simple and peaceful life can offer rich encounters with the ultimate if we don't pre-judge how God will be made manifest to us. Not knowing how God will appear *in us* and *before us* we must move ahead with what seems good and look everywhere to see what good may be happening right in front of us almost without our noticing it. Let me offer a couple of examples.

Several years ago on television in Ireland there was a show which was called "The Gay Byrne Hour." Some loved it, some hated it but almost everyone watched it. One of the special features of the show around Christmas time was the live Christmas Eve broadcast held outside on Grafton Street (the main road running through Dublin). During this particular show the host would invite people to sing, tell stories, and interact with him. One Christmas, knowing this was to happen, a young woman convinced her friend to go with her to Grafton Street and try to get on the show. She had a good voice and thought it would be fun to test her talent in a live broadcast, never expecting the chance would present itself.

So, she and her friend went. Then, much to her surprise and delight, she was chosen out of the crowd and asked if she would be interested in telling a story or singing something. She said she would and she started singing "O Holy Night." People who were present said that as she began to sing, all of Grafton Street went silent. One person living in Ireland at the time claimed to me that he felt almost all of Ireland went silent.[9] One voice. No expectations. A profound impact. The *unexpected* hand of God in the *ordinary*. Never could this woman have expected the impact she would have. We can't predict the hour we will be called or how God will call us to be a light for others.

The same can be said of the possibilities in the world for us to experience God in others. This was particularly brought across to me at the conclusion of the liturgy celebrated to mark the bicentennial of the Baltimore Carmel—the oldest carmel in the United States. As the liturgy was drawing to a close, the choir began to sing the Hallelujah Chorus of Handel's Messiah. As I listened to them, I was distracted by some peripheral motion. When I looked over to the side I could see that there was a group of hearing-impaired persons who had come to the celebration. And much to my surprise, their leader knew the words to the chorus and was singing it for those in front of him. Then, of even greater surprise to me, the hearing impaired section of the congregation began to sign it with him. (They knew it too!) As I watched them and heard the choir in the background, I was overwhelmed. After it was over I knew that I had never heard nor been as moved by Handel's work as I was at this moment. The hand of God had moved me to hear the Spirit in a new way.

Too often we say God is missing—both in ourselves and in the world. Too frequently we lose both our spiritual and our psychological perspective and wish that something dramatic would return it to us. Yet, more often than not, our epiphanies rely on the ordinary. It is in being awake to the presence of God both in our movements toward maturity and affiliation, and toward obedience and solidarity, that the possibilities which are now hidden from us can be revealed. Knowing this is the gift of *understanding*; practicing it everyday is openness to the gift of *insight*. There is a world of difference between these two gifts, and how we experience life will surely prove this to us.

4

Reaching Out . . .
Without Being Pulled Down

*But those who identify the kingdom of God with heaven
are mistaken; the kingdom means rather the spiritual life,
which begins in this life by faith, and in which we grow
deeply as we progress in constant faith.*[1]
—John Calvin on John 3:3

Most committed Christians would not quibble with the claim
that involvement in modern ministry can be quite dangerous to
one's emotional and spiritual health. When this statement was
made in a recent mixed class of new seminary students and experienced pastors returning for a Th.M. degree, the seminary students
wrote it down, the Th.M. students just nodded their heads affirmatively. Today's involved Christians are walking "a narrow and
winding road between banality and crucifixion."[2] And although the
literature on stress and burnout (which was so popular several years
ago) has faded from the scene, the question for many of us who wish
to be meaningfully involved in ministerial life still remains: "While
we are extending our warmth to others, how do we prevent our *own*
emotional flame from burning out in the process?"[3]

Possibly one of the reasons this question remains a pressing
one is that while a knowledge of the psychology of stress is important (not to employ this information would be foolish), at a deeper

level, a more significant way of balancing and strengthening one's efforts to care for others in need is by taking the necessary steps to try to center them spiritually.[4] One's efforts and actions on behalf of others must be based *not* on one's *own* abilities or knowledge, but instead on a *covenantal spirituality*. This is a radical openness to a prayerful relationship with the presence of God in oneself, in others, and in those quiet honest encounters with the Lord in silence and solitude.[5]

When people approach us for help, no matter what they are seeking, they are also really—to some degree—saying: "[Please,] we would like to see Jesus."[6] And, as in the time of the original apostles, when we recognize this significant element in the questions people are asking, we naturally feel overwhelmed and turn to Jesus as they did. And, as in the case of the historical Jesus, the Lord today returns the burden to us, giving us the command: "You give them something to eat."[7] The crucial question for us at a time like this is: What in fact do we have to give those who come to us for spiritual food? Our reply to this question may well determine whether our response will be truly authentic, and whether, in the long run, we will be able to sustain "the good fight" or burn out before the job is done.

What we have available when people approach us certainly can and should include a knowledge of sacred scripture, theology, psychology, and the other gifts we have been given to build up community. However, above all, we must also be able to share a sense of the passion and perspective of Christ. And this is primarily centered in only one place: in a covenantal spirituality based on a deep living faith received from God. Anything less than this, as John Wesley notes in the following statement, falls short of the mark

> I had a sort of faith during my early life. But devils also have a sort of faith. Still, neither they nor I received the faith of the covenant of promise. Even the apostles had a sort of faith when

they were first with Jesus in Cana. Then and there, they "believed in him" in a way. But they did not yet have the faith
which overcomes the world.[8]

Consequently, we must take the necessary steps to continually
develop our spiritual openness so that our prayer life doesn't remain
narrow and our daily prayerful interactions with others don't become distorted. Given this, and as a way to both nurture a radical
relationship with the living God and to show gratitude to the Lord
for the gift of grace (so that we don't unconsciously make Christian
action into just another performance-oriented activity), I would like
to suggest five areas which are worthy of further attention in our
lives. They are areas which I believe are important in order to help
us avoid modeling our own lives in accord with a world that glorifies
success. Instead, attending to them can help us recall our covenant
with God and respond to life in *obedience to God* and *solidarity
with others.*

In covering these areas, I will first reflect on how they can feed
a vital spiritual life and help us to avoid the dangerous extremes of
narrow quietism and undisciplined activism. Following this, I will
offer several practical recommendations for consideration. The five
areas I wish to treat are: (1) *self-awareness;* (2) *spiritual exegesis;* (3)
acts of love; (4) *feedback from others;* (5) *quiet prayer.*

Self-Awareness

A sound covenantal spirituality is based in part on self-
knowledge. There must be a willingness to face the natural resistances we have to uncovering unpleasant truths about ourselves and
to deal with the more subtle "sins of adaptation" that occur when
we unconsciously seek to make the Christian message comfortable.

As we can see in the following comment, John Calvin strongly
believed in self-knowledge:

With good reason the ancient proverb [Know thyself] strongly
recommended knowledge of self. For if it is considered dis-
graceful for us not to know all that pertains to the business of
human life, even more detestable is our ignorance of ourselves,
by which, when making decisions in necessary matters, we
miserably deceive and even blind ourselves.[9]

In addition, Calvin recognized that true self-knowledge was
not self-worship, as some of the current narcissistic self-help literature would have us believe. Instead, it is the font of true humility. In
his commentary on Isaiah 6:5, he noted: "Until God reveals himself
to us, we do not think we are [persons] . . . we think we are gods; but
when we have seen God, then we begin to feel and know what we
are. Hence springs true humility, which consists in this, that a
[person] make no claim for himself [herself], and depend wholly
on God."[10]

And so, in the spirit of 1 Corinthians 12, self-awareness is
important for us not only to begin to appreciate the gifts we are
given, but also to recognize the *source* of those gifts and how we are
blocking them from reaching full development, because "from a
psychological perspective, sin is primarily the result of denying,
ignoring, or worshiping our personality instead of nurturing it in
light of the gospel call to respond in faith, hope, and love."[11]

But wanting self-knowledge and attaining it are obviously two
very radically different things. As Thoreau aptly recognized: "It is
as hard to see oneself as to look backwards without turning
round."[12] Still, try we must to understand ourselves because, as the
Talmudic saying accurately points out: "We do not see things as
they are; we see things as we are."

To try to understand ourselves is not easy then. I believe we
must have discipline and courage, be specific in our daily reflections, and never forget God's love. *Discipline* is essential because
we must take out time during and at the end of the day to monitor
our feelings, thoughts, images, and actions to see what themes arise

for us; otherwise we will just keep moving (maybe in a rut, maybe in the wrong direction—much evil in this world has been done in the name of good!). Taking out even a few minutes for this purpose is not easy though, not only because time is precious, but also because we tend to waste so much of it on action without reflection. When one U.S. senator was asked what was the greatest challenge facing the senate today, he quickly responded: "Not enough time to think." Today, the same can be said of the church and its committed members.

In line with this, one must have the courage to see with a sense of equanimity our good and bad motivations, our mature and immature agendas and attitudes. Only then can our effort at self-knowledge move with courage to a sense of discovery and hope.

In undertaking self-examination, one must remember to be detailed. *Specific interactions* need to be monitored so one can avoid hiding behind broad condemnations of others or vague personal repentances. These lead to goals that seldom translate into concrete actions.

And, finally, reflection must be done before a *loving God.* If it is not, our self-awareness may well become a form of self-condemnation. This, in turn will only lay the foundation for chronic, debilitating guilt or eventual denial instead of spiritual and psychological progress. The simple reason for this is that no one of us likes to look at negative things that we believe will make us feel bad. As a result, behavior we wince at usually turns into behavior that we wink at.[13]

Guilt certainly has a proper prophetic place in all our lives; it helps to break through the crust of self-righteousness that we all have at some point or other. However, guilt cannot serve as a sustaining force for very long. While guilt pushes us to do something good because it is right, only love can continually encourage us to do the right thing because it is natural.[14]

Given this, the spiritual axiom which seems to be a good summary of the attitude needed in self-examination is: *Be clear and be not afraid, for you are loved by God.* With this model to guide us, we can seek clarity and do it without fear because, despite our sin, God loves us and has called us friends.[15] So, with this love (based on a deep appreciation of the cross, resurrection, and ministry of Christ), we can, with God's grace, cut through such major enemies of self-awareness as denial, self-reliance, fear of rejection, undue concern with our image or success, and preoccupation with the troubles of the world without a sense of the sovereignty of God.

We also need to recognize how an overreliance on works can lead to undisciplined activism and set us up for spiritual and psychological burnout. This happens when we fail to appreciate the perspective that is an outgrowth of a theology of hope built on faith—and faith in God alone!

Accordingly, with an appreciation of the value of self-awareness and the need for it on the part of the committed person (so that his or her Christian action will remain vital, honest, and prophetic), the following steps are suggested as one way to encourage improved self-awareness: (1) take out a pre-established regular time during the day (at noon and in the evening on the way home are often good times) to place yourself in the presence of God for reflection; (2) reflect on how you are feeling, thinking, behaving and imaging yourself (and the world) in light of the call of the gospel to love God, yourself and others; (3) pick specific interactions that stand out (negatively/positively) and see what you can learn from them.

Spiritual Exegesis

Many spiritual leaders have ceased to be surprised by the Bible. The simple reality is that religious people always know how the stories turn out. As a result, the challenge of the Spirit is set aside and the perspective, which might come with an ongoing, actual dialogue with the word, is lost as well.

Many of us, in our effort to become thoroughly familiar on a cognitive level with scripture, have lost Karl Barth's sense that when you are asking the Bible "What is this book saying?" it should answer: "Who is this that is asking?" Still, when the interplay between personal identity and the living word is missing, this sense of an ongoing formation of biblical identity is lost as well. It is no wonder that a number of years ago William Sloan Coffin, in his usual colorful fashion, said: "The Bible is like a mirror. When an ass peers in, don't expect an apostle to peer out."

What can we do about this? Well, the practical recommendation here is to read sacred scripture each day as usual, but at least part of the time do it in the spirit of the practice of *lectio divina*. By that I mean we should: (1) select a few minutes each day to read the scriptures prayerfully and with a sense of expectation and surprise. (Appreciating recent scholarship, for example, a feminist interpretation of the Bible is one way to set the stage in this regard. Such an approach breaks down the common patriarchal modes of imagery and allows us to see more vividly those themes that previously remained in the shadows and were unable to prophetically challenge us. (2) While reading the passages, do a spiritual exegesis, i.e. read the words with love and a sense of discovery until something seems to strike home. (3) Simply sit with that passage as one would with a good friend—not thinking, analyzing (or, heaven forbid, creating a sermon out of it!), but instead remaining in a quiet, listening spirit, so the word can nurture and challenge you.

Acts of Love

Most involved Christians happily hold fast to the belief that: "Faith without works is dead."[16] Rarely have I been consulted by a denomination or parish because their pastoral staff or lay leaders weren't doing *enough*. However, even though this is the case, true acts of love are still hard to find. Acts of compulsion, on the other hand, abound and bind. Most people, especially those in ministry, are unfortunately guilty of that terrible Christian "disease"—

chronic niceness. They don't give with a sense of *mitzvah* (giving without expecting anything in return). They give hoping to please and appease.

Giving with a true sense of detachment is a lost art. More often than not, ministry is mainly done with an overconcern about whether people will perceive one's efforts as successful or charitable, and this attitude is a sure road to ministerial "burnout."

Urban Holmes especially appreciated this theme in his book *Spirituality for Ministry* where he noted: "The opposite of detachment is not compassion, it is seduction."[17] We are seduced by the expectations of others and our own unreasonable expectations rather than the expectations of God. Too often we give without discerning whether or not God is calling us to carry certain crosses. When this occurs, such undisciplined activism may lead to an unnecessary depletion of our resources and a cessation of vital involvement in ministry. Christian masochism is still masochism.

The reasons for such self-destructive actions on the part of ministers are myriad, but certainly they must include concern about what people will think, concern about one's image as an involved Christian. Yet this worrisome attitude about how one looks, and whether one is pleasing others, goes completely counter to Christ's example in his ministry. For nowhere in the New Testament is there evidence of Jesus comparing himself to others or clinging to his divinity. Instead, he was only interested in *obeying* the Father and being in *solidarity* with others.

Jesus knew he was loved; in common parlance, he didn't have a self-esteem problem. *He didn't give to others in order to be loved; he gave because he was in love.* Therefore, one of the most dramatic steps you can take in becoming a person who is more generous with others is to learn to like yourself and to appreciate that you are a special creation of God entirely independent of the world's view. As T.S. Eliot recognizes: "Most of the trouble in the world is caused by people wanting to be important." The reality we should model then is: Because of Christ's love we are *already* important.

In reaching out to others, this need to be important is sometimes disguised; it can be seen under the garb of being liked, or being effective, or being relevant. Yet, trading passion for popularity in ministry results in only short-term rewards. Comfortability and success are never a good substitute for peace. Such peace comes from praying honestly and openly, discerning what God is calling us to do, doing it as best we can, and then not worrying about the results or what people think. To repeat James Fenhagen's important message once again here: "People live cautiously because they pray cautiously."[18]

Ironically, it is the desire to be *both* cautious and involved that encourages burnout, not the very act of involvement in itself. The simple biblical principle here is that one simply can't serve two masters. Jesus didn't say: "It would be nice if you didn't serve two masters." He didn't say: "You should work against the tendency to serve two masters." He was direct; his command was simple: "You *cannot* serve two masters."[19] So, when we try to, we pay the price both psychologically and spiritually.

Having said this, the recommendations I offer for consideration in this area of loving, rather than compulsive, service are: (1) Continually review your motives for reaching out to others. The Ibo of Nigeria have a saying: "It is the heart that gives; the fingers just let go." (2) Seek to respond to the Spirit by lighting the one candle God is asking of you at this moment. Appreciate God's sovereignty rather than trying to change the world alone. (3) Recognize that when your service is leading to depression, despair or anxiety, these "bad fruits" often mean that you have put your hand around something less than God's will (e.g. your desire to look good, be spectacular, be loved by others . . .). (4) Reflect on whether or not you are unconsciously seeking the crosses you would prefer over the ones you fear God might be giving you if your life were less hectic and your giving less compulsive.

Feedback from Others

To grow spiritually and in self-awareness and avoid unnecessarily being pulled down, feedback from others is also essential. Still, even though this is the case, we often back away from this process because we are frightened of what we might hear. This anxiety is an indication once again that we have centered ourselves on something or someone less than God. In addition, it is a sign that we have set ourselves up to filter out the positive and emphasize the negative, to hear praise as a whisper and negative comments as thunder.

As strange as it sounds, one of the greatest challenges of the spiritual life is not to give love but to *receive* it. When we are open to receiving the love that is all around us, we can freely share it with others and hear negative criticism without losing perspective or the ability to give. As John XXIII said many years ago: "Whoever has a heart full of love always has something to share." Or, as one author once aptly observed: "Our communities desperately need justice, non-violence and self-giving love, but they can only be led to it by those who have it in themselves."[20]

Feedback should be sought from colleagues who are "soul friends," those spiritually and psychologically mature persons who are not keyed into success and performance, but are willing to expend the energy necessary to listen to us and learn enough about us to be helpful. When we ask others (as the former mayor of New York Edward Koch used to): "How am I doing?" we should look to them for concrete helpful comments that will lead us closer to God.

Too often after we finish school, with the absence of a ready community of friends and colleagues (as is especially the case for ordained ministers who were together in the seminary), we try to go it alone. This is a mistake. A community of friends and colleagues and a chance for faith sharing as well as an exchange of views and feelings provide a life in the Spirit necessary for a continued commitment to our work with others in need.

In some cases this need not involve a major time commitment. Good can result in an exchange that takes only minutes. For example, I have felt inspired, challenged and loved even after a brief encounter with other faculty members and students over lunch.

Informal and formal teaching and preaching also offer good opportunities for information and important feedback for those of us who have the opportunity to be involved in such activities. As Fred Craddock notes: "Preaching is a vital part of pastoral work in that it permits both the preacher and parishioners to weigh, submit to theological examination, integrate, bring to clarity, and express issues that are scattered through the many pastoral contacts and activities."[21]

Discussions after the class or service give an opportunity not just to hear a simple phrase of delight or dissent by others, but a chance to move more deeply into the word.

With the above points in mind, some practical recommendations in the area of feedback I offer for consideration are to: (1) See God's love and hand in the reactions of others. (2) Accept the love that is already around you so you can be nourished to feel strong enough to bear the brunt of necessary criticism. (3) See the corrections of others as possible doors to a more spiritually vital life and recognize that it is natural to resist change, even good change. We are all apt to be like Peter and wish to set up tents around beliefs and themes which bring us comfortability and respect—but possibly not God.

Quiet Prayer

We ponder the nuances of Jesus' parables so often that sometimes we forget that he was also frequently very direct in his instruction. When this directness occurs, it is both a duty to obey and an opportunity to try to fathom the deep treasure within the simplicity of the message. One such occasion was the command he gave to his disciples to follow his example: "Come away by yourself to a lonely place, and rest awhile."[22]

Since the time of the Lord, this call to "rest in the Lord" (*quies* or *hesychia*) has been emulated by many Christians and most religious leaders. Luther, for example, obeyed this call. We remember him for saying that when he knew he was going to have a very busy day, he would get up even earlier so he could pray longer. He recognized and lived out the desert wisdom maxim: "Prayer quickly straightens out your thoughts."[23] He knew that he needed time to go into his room, shut his door, and pray to the Lord in secret[24] as a way to keep his perspective spiritually centered.

This wisdom is as important today as it was in the time of Christ and in the religiously intense reformation time of Luther. The question then is: Why do we resist giving this time supremacy in our own lives? The answer I offer is that as much as we say we'd like to be filled with the Spirit, we are also frightened of taking on Christ's yoke of peace and perspective because we are unconsciously willful in our desire to control our own destiny.[25] We want to resist the conversion and the prophetic call that may be heard when we are alone without our badge of works and schedule full of distractions.

As Henri Nouwen points out: "Solitude is not a private therapeutic place. Rather it is a place of conversion, the place where the old self dies, the place where the new self is born, the place where the emergence of the new man and new woman occurs."[26] While I agree with Nouwen's point of view, when I think of the frightening opportunity that silence and solitude bring to listen and to be with the Lord, I am even more drawn to the reflection recently offered by Thomas Long of Princeton Theological Seminary on Paul's Damascus experience:

> When [Paul] describes the Damascus road experience in Galatians, he does so not so much in the language of conversion,

but in the classical language of a prophetic call. In other words, the focus is not primarily on something that bubbled up within him, but rather on a claim that came from outside him. He talks less about his becoming alive to Christ than he does about Christ becoming alive to him. To be sure, Paul was transformed by the experience, but before he was transformed, he was transfixed by the presence of the risen Christ. Even in the account of Acts we do not find Paul gliding away from the Damascus road singing the convert's song of a new orientation, "Amazing grace, how sweet the sound. . . . Once I was blind, but now I see." To the contrary, his song could only have been, "Amazing grace, how disturbing the presence . . . once I saw, but now I am blind."[27]

The point is: Paul didn't have God . . . God had Paul! Saul was busy doing "God's work" *as best he knew it* when the Lord made a claim on him and called him to an opposite mission and an identity he could never have come to by himself.

Maybe that is what we are trying to run from when we make a case for not following Christ's simple call to close the door to be in the room alone with God. Maybe we can appreciate to some degree what Metropolitan Anthony of Sourozh means when he says: "To meet God means to enter into the 'cave of the tiger'—it is not a pussy cat you meet—it's a tiger. The realm of God is dangerous."[28]

To say with Samuel, "Speak, Lord. Your servant is listening,"[29] is obviously not easy; it's humbling. As Calvin clearly appreciated: "When we have seen God, then we begin to feel and know what we are. Hence springs true humility, which consists in this, that a [person] make no claim for himself [herself], and depend wholly on God."[30]

Whatever the cost, then, there is no choice if we are to follow Christ's example. Silence and solitude are necessary if we are to hear God's voice. Just as necessary is our willingness to be faithful by giving the Lord the time necessary for quiet prayer each day.

How we pray is of course up to us. Each of us must take off our shoes and meet God on holy ground in our own way. However, the following basic ideas, which most of us learned formally or informally at some time or other early in our religious training, are worth repeating here: (1) Find a quiet place to sit and relax. (2) Put yourself in the presence of a loving God and wrap yourself in gratitude. If you don't have these feelings pray for them as you continue. (3) Take either a centering word (Jesus), or read a few passages from the Bible or a spiritual book. (4) Sit with the spirit of what you have read or quietly repeat the centering word over and over again. If you become aware of anything else or are distracted, just let the issue move through your mind and out. If it persists, then hand it over to God rather than preoccupying yourself with it, which, after all, serves no purpose.[31] (5) Sit quietly like this with the Lord in love for ten or twenty minutes a day on a regular basis and your relationship with God will grow.

Final Comments

As we try to be present and assist family, friends, and others in need, it is quite easy to lose one's way. Certainly the road to Emmaus can be used as a theme all through one's life of Christian service. We are so blind so much of the time. And much of the blindness we have is traced to losing our way spiritually because we have put our hands around our image, our expectation for dramatic results, or our secret expectations that people will especially love us because we are publicly committed to serve Christ and them. We have forgotten the covenant, forgotten grace . . . forgotten God. And unfortunately we have forgotten that no matter how talented we are, we must remember Christ's injunction to the apostles: "With [humanity] it is impossible, but not with God: for with God all things are possible."[32]

One of my seminary students quoted the comment of a colleague who taught him an important lesson. He wrote: "When I left seminary I was very capable, and I went out into ministry relying solely on my own gifts and abilities. God rarely came into my equation. Why should God? I seemed to be doing very well on my own. But then after two or three years of 'successful' ministry, I began to realize that there was something missing at the gut level of what I was doing."

In this chapter we too have been looking for what we may be missing. We have looked at our spirituality—our covenantal relationship with the presence of God. We have sought it in ourselves, others, and in those quiet, solitary, honest encounters with the Lord. We have found it to be essential if we are to continue reaching out to others without being pulled down.

This chapter, as in an earlier one in this book, was essentially about remembering. Remembering what? Remembering the covenant. Remembering grace. Remembering the reason why we desired to reach out to others as Christ did in the first place. With a deep appreciation of our covenantal spirituality we remember God's love, and we join it with ours so we can live out a passionate ministry with our identity in Christ and continue to say boldly and loudly with the Lord: "I have come to send fire on the earth, and how I wish it were already kindled!"[33]

5

A "Month of Perspective":
An Afterword

In this short book I have tried to offer some helpful themes and practical approaches to deal with certain psychological and spiritual difficulties and challenges. After finishing a book, particularly a small work like this one, I often wistfully think: "I wish I could really remember and put into practice some of what I have read here." After receiving an initial draft of the chapter "Reaching Out . . . Without Being Pulled Down" a minister candidly reflected: "I like it and I agree with it; I only wish I had a way of overcoming my resistances to putting the points you made into practice."

Consequently, I have started taking out the time to review each book after I have read it. My feeling is that there is a real value to the principle: better less-read . . . but more remembered. In fact, the contents and themes of this book are products of my taking out the time to review what I have read and the types of things I have experienced in light of such readings. Given this, and to save the reader time, I have reviewed each section of the book in order to glean thirty points which may help lead to the kind of perspective that encourages us to be more obedient to God and in closer solidarity with others without having to carry the unnecessary neurotic crosses which come when caring people become lost in the maze of trying to meet everyone's crazy expectations—including their own!

The thirty short phrases are themes which are meant to serve as a basis for a "month of reflection on perspective." An organized way to reflect on the quotes is to use the following steps:

1. In the morning before beginning the day's activities, read one of the phrases and briefly reflect on it.

2. Recall it several times during the day and see how it is applying to the activities, feelings, thoughts, and images you are having today.

3. And in the evening, in a spirit of thankfulness to God, recall it just before going to bed. If you wish, this is also an ideal time to jot down in the book—in the space provided below the quotes—any reflections you might have with respect to it. (This is optional of course; if it becomes more of a chore than its worth, omit doing it.)

The nice thing about following this approach is that although the process will merely take a few minutes/each day—only one hour or so over a period of a month—many of the basic themes of perspective and the other points that may be keyed off in your own mind will have an opportunity to take root and bear fruit. Some of the points may not turn out to be meaningful. Others may be of only short-term value. Some, hopefully, will prove of lasting use. However, by approaching the material in this way, you will have given the overall theme of perspective a higher profile in your outlook on life. You may be surprised by the results.

The final step, after having finished a month of scattered minutes of reflection, is to take a few more final minutes to see what overall psychological-spiritual theme or paradigm you yourself have come up with in how you wish to lead a life of psychological and spiritual perspective. In other words, what one or two sentences seem to sum up the lessons of perspective and clarity you learned? What one phrase might easily help you to recall the presence of God in your life and quickly bring to mind a healthy attitude in how you approach life—especially in difficult or confusing circumstances?

In the beginning of the book I proposed for myself the theme: *Be clear and be not afraid for you are loved by God.* For me, psychological clarity is possible and desirable because the truth sets me free from the bondage of illusion, and I believe the truth is only really approachable when I feel deeply loved by God. However, each of us is different, so the phrase you will find powerful for you will no doubt be different than mine. A suggested guideline in formulating your theme of perspective is: the phrase should be broad enough to reflect an overall approach or psycho-theological philosophy to meeting life but specific enough to be of use.

———————————   ∽   ———————————

A Month of Spiritual and Psychological Perspective

If therefore your eye is good, your whole body will be good.

—Mt 6:22

Day 1. Spirituality dawns when God becomes as real as the problems and joys we face each day.
(Your reflection at day's end.)

Day 2. "The day is short, the work is great, the laborers are sluggish, the wages are high, and the Master of the house is insistent. It is not your duty to finish the work, but you are not free to neglect it." (Rabbi Tarphon)

Day 3. "People live cautiously because they pray cautiously." (James Fenhagen)

Day 4. "We must be faithful in little things in order to be permitted to hope that God in his grace will also send us faithfulness in great things." (Karl Rahner)

Day 5. "The pious [person] needs no miraculous communication to make him [her] aware of God's presence. . . . His [her] awareness may be overlaid momentarily by some shift in consciousness but it never fades away." (Abraham Heschel)

Day 6. The amount of real trust we have in God is sometimes best measured by the depth of the doubt and the seriousness of the questions with which we are willing to live.

Day 7. By wrapping ourselves in silence, solitude, and gratitude, we can open our hearts in contemplation again and again to perspective and simplicity.

Day 8. As resignation moves toward acceptance, real healing and crisis resolution take place.

Day 9. Spiritual and psychological growth occurs only when insight encourages both our hearts and our minds to give up the "advantage" of staying the same in order to opt for something greater yet unknown.

Day 10. One of the greatest human paradoxes is that we seem to complain the most about a lack of spiritual passion in our lives at the very time when we are willing to gamble the least.

Day 11.   "We all do need some external supports and structures to grow . . . yet true freedom demands that we be free even from the communities and structures that support us. Ultimately there is no friend who can fully understand us, who can walk with us all the way. We must go forward and walk on our own in response to who we are and who we are called to be in God. . . . Everywhere in the world one has to pay for the right to live on one's naked spiritual reserves." (Thomas Merton)

Day 12.   Depression often occurs when we have forgotten to love the presence of God in all living things—including, maybe especially, in ourselves.

Day 13. "Education is the ability to listen to almost anything without losing your temper or self-confidence." (Robert Frost)

Day 14. "The day will come when, after mastering the ether, the winds, the tides, gravity, we shall master the energies of love for God. And then, for the second time in the history of the world, [people] will have made fire [their] servant." (Pierre Teilhard de Chardin)

Day 15. "Remember, that there is meaning beyond absurdity. Know that every deed counts, that every word is power . . . above all, remember that you must build your life as if it were a work of art." (Abraham Heschel)

Day 16. One of the greatest things we can do for others is to learn to *like* ourselves. . . . People with solid self-esteem are less defensive, better able to deal with the negativity and pain of others, and are in a good position to inspire true hope in others.

Day 17. People who know, and are at peace with, themselves always have something to share no matter how difficult the situation turns out to be.

Day 18. Failure can awaken us to life in a much more dramatic way than success ever could.

Day 19.   Faith that doesn't include risk is often a sham.

Day 20.   Although we can encounter God everywhere, one of the best places to meet the Lord is contemplatively in the void.

Day 21. "Looking for God is like seeking a path in a field of snow; if there is no path and you are looking for one, walk across it and there is your path." (Thomas Merton)

Day 22. Our depressive, anxious, stressful feelings are sometimes the result of our putting our psychological and spiritual "hands" around something less than God.

Day 23. "I pray to God to free me of God for God's sake."
(Meister Eckhart)

Day 24. "The opposite of detachment is not compassion, it is
seduction" (Urban Holmes). We are seduced by the expectations of
others and our own unreasonable expectations rather than the expectations of God.

Day 25. Jesus didn't give to others in order to be loved; he gave because he was in love.

Day 26. "Most of the trouble in the world is caused by people wanting to be important." (T.S. Eliot)

Day 27.   One of the greatest challenges of the spiritual life is not to give love but to receive it. When we are open to receiving the love that is all around us, we can freely share it with others and hear negative criticism without losing perspective or the ability to give.

Day 28.   "Solitude is not a private therapeutic place. Rather it is a place of conversion, the place where the old self dies, the place where the new self is born, the place where the emergence of the new man and new woman occurs." (Henri Nouwen)

Day 29. Guilt certainly has a proper prophetic place in all our lives; it helps to break through the crust of self-righteousness that we all have at some point or other. However, guilt cannot serve as a sustaining force for very long; for whereas guilt pushes us to do something good because it is right, only love can continually encourage us to do the right thing because it is natural.

Day 30. "We do not see things as they are; we see things as we are." (The Talmud)

Theme of Spiritual and Psychological Perspective

If anyone loves me, he will keep my word; and my Father will love him and we will make our home with him. . . . Peace I leave with you, my peace I give to you. Let not your heart be troubled, neither let it be afraid.

—Jn 14:23,27

Be clear and be not afraid because you are loved by God. (Your theme)

Notes

1. Be Clear and Be Not Afraid

1. Thomas Merton, *New Seeds of Contemplation*, New York: New Directions, 1961, p. 111.

2. Spiritual Strength

1. Urban Holmes, *Spirituality for Ministry*, San Francisco, Harper and Row, 1982, p. 35.

2. Henri Nouwen, *Clowning in Rome*, New York: Doubleday, 1979, p. 26.

3. Lionel Blue, *Lionel Blue*, Springfield: Templegate, 1987, p. 28.

4. Ibid., p. 24.

5. Abraham Heschel, *Quest for God*, New York: Scribners, 1954.

6. James Fenhagen, *Invitation to Holiness*, San Francisco: Harper and Row, 1985, p. 57.

7. Gerald May, *Will and Spirit*, San Francisco: Harper & Row, 1982.

8. From Maya Angelou's presentation in PBS special on the topic of "Evil."

9. Karl Rahner, *Words of Faith*, New York: Crossroad, 1987, p. 40.

10. Samuel Dresner (ed.), *I Asked for Wonder: A Spiritual Anthology of Abraham Joshua Heschel*, New York: Crossroad, 1986, p. 68.

11. Anthony de Mello, *One Minute Wisdom*, New York: Doubleday, 1986, p. 102.

12. Ibid.

13. William Glasser, *Reality Therapy*, New York: Harper & Row, 1965.

14. Basil Pennington, *Thomas Merton, Brother Monk*, San Francisco: Harper & Row, 1987, pp. 24, 25.

15. Ibid.

16. Quoted by Thomas Merton in *A Vow of Conversation* (edited by Naomi Stone Burton), New York: Farrar, Straus, and Giroux, 1988, p. 9.

17. J. P. Dumbois-Dumee, "Renewal of Prayer," *Lumen Vitae*, 38, 3, 1983, pp. 273–274.

18. Pierre Teilhard de Chardin, *On Love and Happiness*, San Francisco: Harper & Row, 1984, p. 16

3. Enemies of Spiritual and Psychological Perspective

1. Anthony de Mello, *One Minute Wisdom*, New York: Doubleday, 1986, pp. 78, 104, 154.

2. Samuel Dresner (ed.), *I Asked for Wonder*, New York: Crossroad, 1986, p. ix.

3. Thomas Merton, source unknown.

4. James Finley, *Merton's Palace of Nowhere*, Notre Dame: Ave Maria Press, 1978.

5. Alice Walker, *The Color Purple*, New York: Harcourt, Brace and Jovanovich, 1982.

6. From an interview with Thich Nhat Nanh in *Common Boundary*, Nov./Dec. 1989, p. 16.

7. Henri Nouwen, *Making All Things New*, San Francisco: Harper & Row, 1981, p. 33.

8. Maxim Gorky, *Gorky: My Childhood*, London: Penguin, 1966, p. 173.

9. I am grateful to Tommy O'Connor for sharing this experience with me.

4. Reaching Out . . . Without Being Pulled Down

1. John Calvin, *Commentaries*, edited and translated by Joseph Haroutunian and Louise Pettibone Smith, Library of Christian Classics, Vol. 23, Philadelphia: Westminster Press, 1958, p. 138. Italics supplied.

2. M. Scott Peck, "Self-Ministry," *Ministries*, 1, no. 4 (1980), pp. 7, 8.

3. Robert J. Wicks, *Self-Ministry Through Self-Understanding*, Chicago: Loyola University Press, 1990.

4. See bibliography in: Robert J. Wicks, "Countertransference and Burnout," in: Wicks, Robert J., Parsons, R. and Capps, D. (eds.), *Clinical Handbook of Pastoral Counseling*, Mahwah: Paulist, 1985, pp. 76–96.

5. Robert J. Wicks, *Availability: The Problem and the Gift*, Mahwah: Paulist, 1986, p. 1.

6. Jn 12:21.

7. Mk 6:37.

8. John Wesley, *The Nature of Spiritual Growth*, Minneapolis: Bethany, 1977, p. 17.

9. John Calvin, *Institutes of the Christian Religion*, edited by J.T. McNeill, The Library of Christian Classics, Vol. 21, Philadelphia: Westminster, 1960, II, i, p. 1.

10. Ibid., L.i.2. Cf. commentary on Isaiah 6:5.

11. Robert J. Wicks, *Living Simply in an Anxious World*, Mahwah: Paulist, 1988, p. 57.

12. Henry David Thoreau, quoted by W.H. Auden in his Introduction to Dag Hammarskjold's *Markings*, New York: Knopf, 1976, p. ix.

13. Robert J. Wicks, *Availability*, p. 16.

14. Robert J. Wicks, *Living Simply in an Anxious World*, p. 40.

15. Jn 15:14.

16. Jas 2:26.

17. Urban Holmes, *Spirituality for Ministry*, San Francisco: Harper & Row, 1982, p. 150.

18. James Fenhagen, *Invitation to Holiness*, San Francisco: Harper & Row, 1985, p. 57.

19. Mt 6:24.

20. Michael Scanlon, *Inner Healing*, Ramsey: Paulist, 1974, p. 15.

21. Fred Craddock, *Preaching*, Nashville: Abingdon, 1985, p. 40.

22. Mk 1:35.

23. Yushi Nomura, *Desert Wisdom: Sayings of the Desert Fathers*, New York: Doubleday, 1982, p. 32.

24. Mt 6:6.

25. Mt 11:29–30.

26. Henri Nouwen, *Way of the Heart*, New York: Seabury, 1981, p. 18.

27. Thomas G. Long, "Why Are We Here," *Testament*, Vol. 1, No. 1, November 1989, p. 7.

28. Anthony Bloom, *Beginning to Pray*, Ramsey: Paulist Press, 1970, pp. xv–xvi.

29. I Sam 3:10.

30. Louis A. Vos, "The Christian Self-Image," in *Exploring the Heritage of John Calvin*, edited by David Holwerda, Grand Rapids: Baker, 1976, p. 81.

31. Mt 6:27.

32. Mk 10:27.

33. Lk 12:47.